MW01505359

WORLD POLITICAL LEADERS
World Governments Series

Written by Darcy B. Frisina, M.Ed.

GRADES 5 - 8
Reading Levels 3 - 4

Classroom Complete Press

P.O. Box 19729
San Diego, CA 92159
Tel: 1-800-663-3609 / Fax: 1-800-663-3608
Email: service@classroomcompletepress.com

www.classroomcompletepress.com

ISBN-13: 978-1-55319-352-4
ISBN-10: 1-55319-352-0

© 2007

Permission to Reproduce

Critical Thinking Skills

World Political Leaders

Skills For Critical Thinking	Reading Comprehension												Writing Tasks
	Bush	Reagan	Castro	Fox	Peron	Thatcher	Gorbachev	Mandela	Gandhi	Arafat	Zemin	Dalai Lama	
LEVEL 1 Knowledge													
• List Details/Facts		✓					✓	✓		✓			
• Recall Information	✓	✓		✓	✓	✓	✓	✓	✓	✓	✓		
• Match Vocabulary to Definitions		✓	✓	✓	✓		✓			✓	✓	✓	
• Label Maps	✓		✓	✓		✓				✓		✓	
• Recognize Validity (T/F)	✓						✓						
LEVEL 2 Comprehension													
• Summarize		✓			✓	✓	✓		✓	✓			✓
• State Main Idea			✓								✓		
• Describe		✓		✓	✓		✓			✓	✓		
• Interpret			✓					✓					
• Compare/Contrast													✓
LEVEL 3 Application													
• Organize Facts	✓	✓	✓				✓						
• Use Outside Research Tools		✓	✓			✓				✓			✓
• Application to Own Life			✓		✓	✓			✓	✓			
• Apply Vocabulary Words in Sentences	✓					✓			✓				
LEVEL 4 Analysis													
• Draw Conclusions										✓			
• Identify Supporting Evidence				✓	✓	✓			✓	✓			✓
• Make Inferences			✓					✓			✓		
• Identify Relationships										✓			
LEVEL 5 Synthesis													
• Predict			✓							✓			
• Imagine Self Interacting with Subject											✓		
• Suppose	✓							✓	✓		✓		✓
• Create a Plan											✓		
LEVEL 6 Evaluation													
• State and Support an Opinion		✓		✓	✓		✓			✓			
• Evaluate Decisions Made by Subject									✓	✓			✓

Based on Bloom's Taxonomy

Contents

TEACHER GUIDE

- Assessment Rubric 4
- How Is Our Resource Organized? 5
- Bloom's Taxonomy for Reading Comprehension 6
- Vocabulary 6

STUDENT HANDOUTS

- Reading Comprehension
    1. George W. Bush (United States) 7
    2. Ronald Reagan (United States) 10
    3. Fidel Castro (Cuba) 13
    4. Vicente Fox (Mexico) 16
    5. Juan and Eva Peron (Argentina) 19
    6. Margaret Thatcher (United Kingdom) 22
    7. Mikhail Gorbachev (Soviet Union/Russia) 25
    8. Nelson Mandela (South Africa) 28
    9. Indira Gandhi (India) 31
    10. Yasser Arafat (Palestine) 34
    11. Jiang Zemin (China) 37
    12. The Dalai Lama (Tibet) 40
- Writing Tasks 43
- Crossword 46
- Word Search 47
- Comprehension Quiz 48

EASY MARKING™ ANSWER KEY 50
MINI POSTERS 55

FREE! 6 Bonus Activities!

3 EASY STEPS to receive your 6 Bonus Activities!
- Go to our website:
  www.classroomcompletepress.com\bonus
- Enter item CC5761
- Enter pass code CC5761D

Assessment Rubric

• •

World Political Leaders

Student's Name: _____   Assignment: _____   Level: _____

	Level 1	Level 2	Level 3	Level 4
Understanding of Basic Concepts	Demonstrates a limited understanding of concepts. Requires teacher intervention.	Demonstrates a basic understanding of concepts. Requires little teacher intervention.	Demonstrates a good understanding of concepts. Requires no teacher intervention.	Demonstrates a thorough understanding of concepts. Requires no teacher intervention.
Understanding of Leader's Regional Impact	Limited understanding of leader's regional impact demonstrated in activity responses.	Some understanding of leader's regional impact demonstrated in activity responses.	Satisfactory level of understanding of leader's regional impact demonstrated in activity responses.	Solid understanding of leader's regional impact demonstrated in activity responses.
Understanding of Leader's Global Impact	Limited understanding of leader's global impact demonstrated in activity responses.	Some understanding of leader's global impact demonstrated in activity responses.	Satisfactory level of understanding of leader's global impact demonstrated in activity responses.	Solid understanding of leader's global impact demonstrated in activity responses.
Identifies Countries & Regions Impacted by Leader on a World Map	Requires significant teacher intervention in order to identify countries and regions studied.	Requires little teacher intervention in order to identify countries and regions studied.	Identifies countries and regions studied with no teacher intervention.	Identifies countries and regions studied perfectly with no teacher intervention.

STRENGTHS:

WEAKNESSES:

NEXT STEPS:

Teacher Guide

Our resource has been created for ease of use by both *TEACHERS* and *STUDENTS* alike.

Introduction

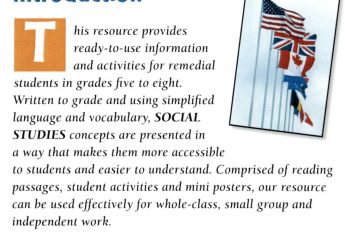

This resource provides ready-to-use information and activities for remedial students in grades five to eight. Written to grade and using simplified language and vocabulary, **SOCIAL STUDIES** concepts are presented in a way that makes them more accessible to students and easier to understand. Comprised of reading passages, student activities and mini posters, our resource can be used effectively for whole-class, small group and independent work.

How Is Our Resource Organized?

STUDENT HANDOUTS

Reading passages and **activities** (in the form of reproducible worksheets) make up the majority of our resource. The reading passages present important grade-appropriate information and concepts related to the topic. Included in each passage are one or more embedded questions that ensure students are actually reading and understanding the content.

For each reading passage there are BEFORE YOU READ activities and AFTER YOU READ activities. As with the reading passages, the related activities are written using a remedial level of language.

- The BEFORE YOU READ activities prepare students for reading by setting a purpose for reading. They stimulate background knowledge and experience, and guide students to make connections between what they know and what they will learn. Important concepts and vocabulary from the reading passage are also presented.

- The AFTER YOU READ activities check students' comprehension of the concepts presented in the reading passage and extend their learning. Students are asked to give thoughtful consideration of the reading passage through creative and evaluative short-answer questions, research, and extension activities.

Writing Tasks are included to further develop students' thinking skills and understanding of the concepts. The **Assessment Rubric** (*page 4*) is a useful tool for evaluating students' responses to many of the activities in our resource. The **Comprehension Quiz** (*page 48*) can be used for either a follow-up review or assessment at the completion of the unit.

PICTURE CUES

Our resource contains three main types of pages, each with a different purpose and use. A Picture Cue at the top of each page shows, at a glance, what the page is for.

 Teacher Guide
- Information and tools for the teacher

 Student Handouts
- Reproducible worksheets and activities

 Easy Marking™ Answer Key
- Answers for student activities

EASY MARKING™ ANSWER KEY

Marking students' worksheets is fast and easy with this **Answer Key**. Answers are listed in columns – just line up the column with its corresponding worksheet, as shown, and see how every question matches up with its answer!

Every question matches up with its answer!

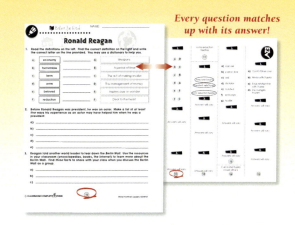

Bloom's Taxonomy

Our resource is an effective tool for any SOCIAL STUDIES PROGRAM.

Bloom's Taxonomy* for Reading Comprehension

The activities in our resource engage and build the full range of thinking skills that are essential for students' reading comprehension and understanding of important social studies concepts. Based on the six levels of thinking in Bloom's Taxonomy, and using language at a remedial level, information and questions are given that challenge students to not only recall what they have read, but move beyond this to understand the text and concepts through higher-order thinking. By using higher-order skills of application, analysis, synthesis and evaluation, students become active readers, drawing more meaning from the text, attaining a greater understanding of concepts, and applying and extending their learning in more sophisticated ways.

Our resource, therefore, is an effective tool for any Social Studies program. Whether it is used in whole or in part, or adapted to meet individual student needs, our resource provides teachers with essential information and questions to ask, inspiring students' interest, creativity, and promoting meaningful learning.

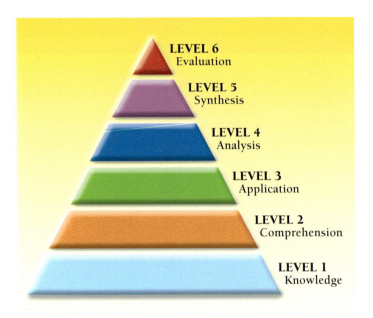

LEVEL 6 Evaluation
LEVEL 5 Synthesis
LEVEL 4 Analysis
LEVEL 3 Application
LEVEL 2 Comprehension
LEVEL 1 Knowledge

BLOOM'S TAXONOMY: 6 LEVELS OF THINKING

Bloom's Taxonomy is a widely used tool by educators for classifying learning objectives, and is based on the work of Benjamin Bloom.

Vocabulary

highjack	terrorist	course	conflict	overthrow	controversial
disbanding	economy	formidable	term	arms	beloved
reduction	embargo	aid	hostile	dictator	personable
isolated	oppose	operations	corrupt	lax	stabilize
immigration	summit	eliminate	wealthy	recognized	organization
ambitious	linked	fled	allies	negotiated	apartheid
release	published	collapsed	citizens	goods	shortage
coup	activist	resistance	treason	convicted	epidemic
surplus	export	threat	fraud	assassinate	figure
liberation	rightfully	notable	hostage	decade	roles
commission	nation	standard	reincarnated	groomed	asylum
restore	waste				

NAME: _____

George W. Bush

1. **Complete each sentence with a word from the list. Use a dictionary to help you.**

highjack	course	overthrow	disbanding
terrorist	conflict	controversial	

  a) The party began _____ after the cake was served.

  b) Paul and Ron are no longer friends because of a _____.

  c) A _____ was caught before he could hurt anyone.

  d) The people got together to _____ the unfair king.

  e) We used a map to decide our _____ to the city.

  f) The end of the game was _____ because the player may have been out of bounds.

  g) Two people tried to _____ the car, but were stopped by the police.

2. **The map has arrows pointing at three countries: the United States, Afghanistan, and Iraq. Using colored pencils, follow the directions below.**

  a) Color the United States **red.**   **b)** Color Afghanistan **blue.**   **c)** Color Iraq **green.**

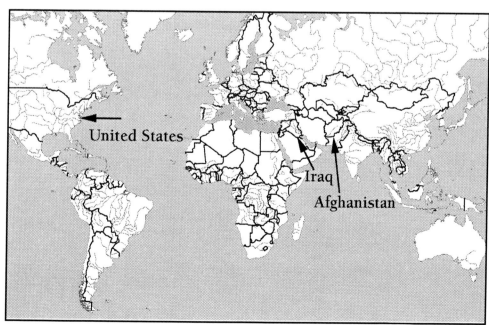

George W. Bush

George W. Bush was born on July 6, 1946. He is the 43rd President of the United States. His father, George Bush Sr., was the 41st President of the United States.

On September 11, 2001, Bush was visiting an elementary school when he learned that the Pentagon and the World Trade Center were attacked. Several people **highjacked** planes and flew them into the buildings. Thousands of people died that day.

This event set the **course** of his Presidency. Bush realized that the people of the world were not safe from **terrorists**. He decided to start a global war on terrorism. In 2001, Bush directed troops to invade Afghanistan, a country in central Asia. The purpose of this **conflict** was to **overthrow** the Taliban, a terrorist group.

Why did the United States invade Afghanistan?

_____

_____

_____

After **disbanding** the Taliban and helping the people of Afghanistan develop a democratic government, Bush focused on another country. In 2003, the U.S. military invaded Iraq. Bush wanted to help spread **democracy** in the Middle East. He also worried that terrorists would be able to get weapons from the Iraqi government and their leader, Saddam Hussein.

Bush's efforts in Iraq were **controversial**, but have had success. Saddam Hussein was captured and found guilty by an Iraqi court of crimes against his own people. Elections were held in 2005 to bring peace to the country and approve a constitution. Saddam Hussein was executed in Baghdad, Iraq by hanging on December 30, 2006.

George W. Bush

1. **Circle** the word **TRUE** if the statement is TRUE **or** **Circle** the word **FALSE** if it is FALSE.

   a) President Bush decided to send troops to Afghanistan to help the Taliban.

        TRUE   **FALSE**

   b) President Bush was worried that terrorists could get guns in Iraq.

        TRUE   **FALSE**

   c) Saddam Hussein helped spread democracy in the Middle East.

        TRUE   **FALSE**

   d) Elections were held in Iraq to help approve a constitution.

        TRUE   **FALSE**

2. **Place the following *events* on the timeline below.**

Events:
  a) Elections were held in Iraq.
  b) Saddam Hussein was found guilty.
  c) The U.S. was attacked on September 11, 2001.
  d) Troops were sent to Afghanistan.
  e) Troops were sent to Iraq.

3. George Bush was also the **Governor of Texas**. In your own words, tell what you would do if you were governor of your state. How could you improve the state in which you live? Your answer should be two to three sentences.

_____

_____

_____

NAME: _____

Ronald Reagan

1. **Read the definitions on the left. Find the correct definition on the right and write the correct letter on the line provided. You may use a dictionary to help you.**

a economy	_____	**A**	Weapons
b formidable	_____	**B**	A period of time
c term	_____	**C**	The act of making smaller
d arms	_____	**D**	The management of money
e beloved	_____	**E**	Inspires awe or wonder
f reduction	_____	**F**	Dear to the heart

2. **Before Ronald Reagan was president, he was an** *actor.* **Make a list of** *at least five* **ways his experience as an actor may have helped him when he was a president.**

a) _____

b) _____

c) _____

d) _____

e) _____

3. **Reagan told another world leader to tear down the** *Berlin Wall.* **Use the resources in your classroom (encyclopedias, books, the Internet) to learn more about the Berlin Wall. Find** *three* **facts to share with your class when you discuss the Berlin Wall as a group.**

a) _____

b) _____

c) _____

Ronald Reagan

Ronald Reagan was the 40th President of the United States. Before he was elected, Reagan had two very different jobs. He was a very famous movie actor in Hollywood. After he stopped acting, Reagan was also the Governor of California.

Reagan earned the nickname "The Great Communicator" because he was able to deliver speeches in a personal manner even in formal settings. He was also known to have a quick sense of humor and a positive attitude.

Reagan was also a **formidable** world leader. His presidency occurred during the Cold War, a time in history when the U.S. and Russia were struggling to get along. He began his **term** by starting an **arms race** with Russia. He knew that Russia would run out of money before the U.S. When this happened, Reagan signed a series of arms **reduction** treaties with Russia. This was an important first step that helped end the Cold War.

STOP — **How did the arms race help bring an end to the Cold War?**

_____

_____

The presidents before Reagan were unsuccessful in ending the Cold War because they tried to ignore the problem. Reagan confronted Russia head-on, even working with Russia to find common ground. Towards the end of his presidency, Reagan visited Mikhail Gorbachev, the leader of Russia. In a very famous speech, Reagan told Gorbachev to "...tear down this wall", referring to the Berlin Wall, a symbol of the Cold War.

Reagan was a rare world leader who was **beloved** by many of the people he touched worldwide. He is remembered as a positive influence on the world.

Ronald Reagan

1. Below is a list of five events. (Circle) the **three** events that occurred as a **result** of Ronald Reagan's leadership.

   The Berlin Wall is built in Germany.
   The arms race begins.
   A U.S. president visits Russia.
   The U.S. ignores Russia.
   The U.S. and Russia sign arms reduction treaties.

2. In your own words, explain how Ronald Reagan **ended** the arms race with Russia.

   _____

   _____

3. Reagan was well-liked worldwide. In **your opinion**, why do you think so many people liked Ronald Reagan? Your answer should be two to three sentences. Use examples from the passage to support your opinion.

   _____

   _____

   _____

4. Ronald Reagan was known as a good speaker. He once said, **"All great change in America begins at the dinner table."** Describe what this quote means. Give examples from your own dinner table to support your explanation. Your answer should be two to three sentences.

   _____

   _____

   _____

NAME: _____

Fidel Castro

1. **Write each word from the list beside its correct meaning. Use a dictionary to help you.**

embargo	hostile	personable	oppose
aid	dictator	isolated	

a) _____ Act against

b) _____ Well-liked

c) _____ Help

d) _____ A leader who rules with total power

e) _____ Separate from everyone else

f) _____ A government order that does not allow trade

g) _____ Angry towards

2. **The U.S. has an *embargo* against Cuba. What if your country had an embargo placed on it? Imagine what your country would be like if other countries would not trade with your country. Make a list of *five* things you could not have if your country was not allowed to trade.**

a) _____

b) _____

c) _____

d) _____

e) _____

3. **Locate Cuba on the map below. Next, locate the southernmost tip of Florida. Estimate the *distance* between Cuba and the U.S. Write your estimate in the box below.**

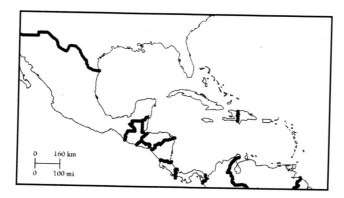

Fidel Castro

Fidel Castro became the leader of Cuba after leading the Cuban Revolution. He helped remove another leader from office during this **revolution**. After taking over the government, Castro has led Cuba for over forty years.

Cuba is a small island less than 100 miles from the southern tip of Florida. However, U.S. citizens are not allowed to travel to Cuba and the United States will not trade with Cuba. In fact, the U.S. has had an **embargo** against Cuba for over forty years.

Castro worked closely with Russian leaders until the end of the Cold War. Both countries had Communist governments. This was a serious threat to the United States.

U.S. leaders worried because they thought that Cuba would **aid** Russia in attack against the U.S. When the Cold War ended, Cuba and Russia ended their close relationship, but the relationship between the U.S. and Cuba remained openly **hostile**.

STOP

Why did U.S. leaders consider Cuba to be a serious threat?

_____

_____

People have many different opinions about Fidel Castro as a leader. Some people believe he is a **personable** leader. Other people believe he is a **dictator.** He has been accused of killing people who oppose him, but others consider Castro to be a hero.

Cuba remains somewhat **isolated** from the rest of the world. Cuba's **economy** has suffered since the end of the Cold War. They are now trying to attract tourists, but U.S. citizens still cannot travel to Cuba.

After You Read 📖

Fidel Castro

1. **Read the following four events. Write them in the correct order on the lines below, starting with the earliest event.**

Castro works closely with Russia.
Cuba encourages tourism.
Castro takes over after the Cuban Revolution.
Castro ends his close relationship with Russia.

a) _____

b) _____

c) _____

d) _____

2. **In your own words, explain why people have so many different *opinions* about Fidel Castro.**

_____

_____

_____

3. **What do you think would happen if the U.S. *lifted* the embargo against Cuba?**

_____

_____

_____

4. **Using the computers and other resources in your classroom, find *four facts* about Cuba. List those facts on the lines provided below.**

a) _____

b) _____

c) _____

d) _____

Vicente Fox

1. **Read the definitions on the left. Find the correct definition on the right. Write the correct letter on the line provided. You may use a dictionary to help you.**

a operations	_____	**A** Not firm or strict
b corrupt	_____	**B** A meeting of leaders
c lax	_____	**C** Daily work
d stabilize	_____	**D** The act of moving to another country
e immigration	_____	**E** To turn from good to bad
f summit	_____	**F** To keep from changing

2. **The map has arrows pointing at three countries: the United States, Cuba, and Mexico. Using colored pencils, follow the directions below.**

a) Color the United States **red.**   b) Color Cuba **blue.**   c) Color Mexico **green.**

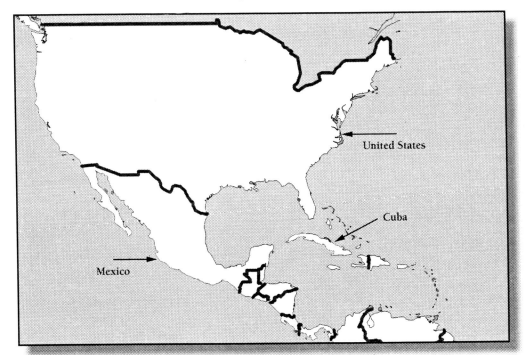

NAME: _____

Vicente Fox

V icente Fox was the 72nd President of Mexico. He was born on July 2, 1942 in Mexico City, but he grew up on a ranch in the country. He moved back to the city when he attended college.

Vicente Fox did not start out wanting to be a politician. After he finished college, Fox started working for Coca-Cola. He started at the bottom, and then was put in charge of **operations** in Mexico. Eventually, he was in charge of Coca-Cola's operations in all of Latin America.

When Fox became President, he decided to fix the problems he saw in the Mexican government. Mexico had the reputation of being **corrupt** and too **lax** on drugs. Fox worked to stop corruption within the Mexican government. He also helped create new laws that made it harder to buy and sell drugs.

What two problems did Fox try to fix when he became President?

_____

_____

Before Fox took office, Mexico was not very involved in world politics. They had a strict rule that said Mexico should not criticize how other governments decide to run their countries. Fox decided to increase Mexico's involvement in world politics.

Fox worked with the U.S. to try to control open **immigration** between the Mexico-U.S. borders. George W. Bush supported these discussions, but no new laws were passed in the U.S.

Fox also worked with other Latin American countries. Mexico held several international **summits** to talk about global issues. Guests included Fidel Castro and George W. Bush. The two leaders were not in the same room at the same time, but Fox wanted to help the two leaders work together.

Vicente Fox

1. Below is a list of four events. (Circle) the *three* events that occurred as a result of Vicente Fox's leadership.

    Fox works with both Bush and Castro.

    Mexico becomes less involved in world politics.

    The U.S and Mexico talk about immigration.

    It is harder to buy and sell drugs in Mexico.

2. Answer each question below in a complete sentence.

    a) What company did Fox work for before he became a politician?

    _____

    b) What was Mexico's opinion about being involved in world politics before Fox?

    _____

    c) Why did Fox try to work with George W. Bush?

    _____

3. Mexico and the United States share a large border. Do you think the border should be *open?* This would mean that people would be able to travel back and forth whenever they want. Your answer should be two to three sentences.

    _____

    _____

    _____

    _____

 Before You Read

Juan and Eva Peron

1. **Write each word from the list beside its correct meaning. Use a dictionary to help you.**

eliminate fled linked	recognized wealthy	ambitious organization

a) _____ Group

b) _____ To get rid of

c) _____ Connected

d) _____ Rich

e) _____ Ran away from

f) _____ Noticed as

g) _____ Wanting control

2. **The Perons worked hard in order to try to help the poor people of their country. List *five* ways in which your country could help its poor people.**

a) _____

b) _____

c) _____

d) _____

e) _____

Juan and Eva Peron

Juan   **Eva Peron**

Juan Peron was a three time President of Argentina. His wife, Eva, was a powerful leader who worked with her husband. They are still very popular figures in Argentina today.

Before he became President, Juan was a colonel in the military, Minister of War, and Vice-President of Argentina. The Perons had several goals that they worked towards together during his Presidency. They wanted to **eliminate** poverty. They also wanted to give power to the working class. Their goals angered the **wealthy** people who did not want to see the working class get richer.

STOP

Why were the wealthy people of Argentina unhappy with the Perons?

_____

_____

_____

Eva Peron was one of the most powerful women of her time. She was **recognized** as a leader within her husband's **organization**. Eva was a very **ambitious** woman. She traveled to Europe on the "Rainbow Tour". On the tour, she met with many European leaders.

When Juan Peron ran for a second time, Eva wanted to be his Vice-President. The military was against the idea of a woman as Vice-President. Besides, Eva quickly became too sick for the job. She died shortly after her husband won the election.

Juan and Eva Peron were **controversial** leaders. Many people loved them. Other people accused them of spending too much money. The Perons have also been **linked** to former Nazis. Many former Nazis **fled** to Argentina.

The Perons are still considered to be heroes by many in Argentina.

NAME: _____

Juan and Eva Peron

1. The Perons worked hard to improve the lives of people in Argentina. List the *two* goals the Perons worked together to achieve.

    a) _____

    b) _____

2. Describe the *purpose* of the "Rainbow Tour". Answer in a complete sentence.

    _____

    _____

3. Eva Peron wanted to be the Vice-President of Argentina. In your own words, explain the *two* reasons why Eva could not have the job. Your answer should be three to four sentences.

    _____

    _____

    _____

    _____

4. Would you vote for a woman to lead your country? Why or why not? Answer in a complete sentence.

    _____

    _____

    _____

Margaret Thatcher

1. Complete each sentence with a word from the list. Use a dictionary to help you.

allies	apartheid	published
negotiated	release	

a) We watched the zookeeper _____ the lion from the cage.

b) The book was _____ a year later.

c) People were upset by _____ and wanted everyone to be treated equally.

d) Canada and the United States are _____.

e) A new deal was _____ between the two boys.

---

2. Using the resources in your classroom, list the *four countries* in the United Kingdom.

a) _____

_____

b) _____

_____

c) _____

_____

d) _____

_____

3. On the map below, *label* the four countries that are the United Kingdom.

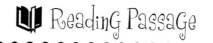 Reading Passage

Margaret Thatcher

Margaret Thatcher was the Prime Minister of the United Kingdom for over ten years. She was the first woman Prime Minister. She is called "The Iron Lady of British Politics" because she was known for being strong and intelligent.

Thatcher often worked closely with Ronald Reagan. The two leaders were **allies** on many international issues. Thatcher helped end the Cold War. She **negotiated** talks with Reagan and the leader of Russia. She helped bring the two leaders together to work out their differences.

She was also interested in other global issues. Thatcher invited leaders from South Africa to talk about ending **apartheid.** She tried to convince the leaders to **release** Nelson Mandela from prison. They did not listen to her advice.

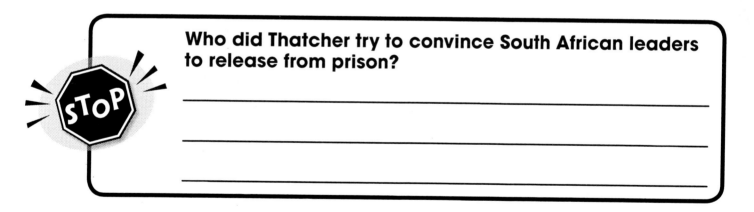

Who did Thatcher try to convince South African leaders to release from prison?

_____

_____

_____

Before she became a politician, Margaret Thatcher was a **chemist.** She helped invent the first soft-serve ice cream. She became involved in saving the environment because of her love of science. She was one of the first world leaders to talk about global warming and acid rain.

Margaret Thatcher has remained active in world politics since leaving office. She has also **published** several books discussing her opinions on world politics.

NAME: _____

Margaret Thatcher

1. **Complete each question below in a complete sentence.**

   a) How did Margaret Thatcher help end the **Cold War?**

   _____

   _____

   b) What were the **two** reasons why Thatcher met with South African leaders?

   _____

   _____

2. Margaret Thatcher worked to help the environment. Choose either **global warming** or **acid rain.** Use the resources in your classroom to learn **five facts** about the issue you have chosen.

   a) _____

   b) _____

   c) _____

   d) _____

   e) _____

3. Thatcher once said, **"You may have to fight a battle more than once to win it."** In two to three sentences, describe a time when you had to keep trying in order to reach a goal.

   _____

   _____

   _____

   _____

NAME: _____

Mikhail Gorbachev

1. Write each word from the list beside its correct meaning. Use a dictionary to help you.

collapsed	goods	coup	citizens	shortage

_____ **a)** Items that can be purchased

_____ **b)** Forceful takeover

_____ **c)** Not enough

_____ **d)** Fell apart

_____ **e)** People who live in a country

2. List *three* facts you have already learned about the Cold War.

a) _____

b) _____

c) _____

3. Russia is one of the countries that were involved in the Cold War. You have read about three other countries also involved in the Cold War. Name the *three* other countries below.

a) _____

b) _____

c) _____

Mikhail Gorbachev

Mikhail Gorbachev was the last leader of the Soviet Union (Russia) before it **collapsed**. He was also the first elected President of the Soviet Union.

Gorbachev worked with Reagan and Thatcher to end the Cold War. He developed close relationships with both leaders. Gorbachev and Reagan met many times to **eliminate** many nuclear weapons. This helped end the arms race and the Cold War.

Gorbachev wanted to improve the lives of his citizens. He allowed freedom of speech, which was against the law before. He allowed people to open and own their own businesses. Before he made this change, businesses and stores were owned by the government.

How did Gorbachev change businesses?

_____

_____

_____

He also held the first election in his country since the Cold War. He was voted the first President of the Soviet Union.

Gorbachev also opened his country to Western goods. This allowed free trade and let people have more choices. He helped to end food **shortages** and gave his people greater freedom. People decided that they liked having choices. They wanted even more freedom. This led to the collapse of his country.

Mikhail Gorbachev left the government after a **coup.** He is now very active in environmental issues. He was given the Nobel Peace Prize because of his efforts to improve his country and the world.

NAME: _____

Mikhail Gorbachev

1. Circle the word **TRUE** if the statement is TRUE **or** Circle the word **FALSE** if it is FALSE.

a) Gorbachev worked with Castro to help end the Cold War.

TRUE   FALSE

b) Gorbachev worked with Reagan to eliminate some nuclear weapons.

TRUE   FALSE

c) Gorbachev did not allow citizens to own their own businesses.

TRUE   FALSE

d) Freedom of speech was made legal.

TRUE   FALSE

e) Gorbachev is still active in environmental issues.

TRUE   FALSE

2. In your own words, **summarize** how people in Russia reacted to their new freedoms.

_____

_____

_____

_____

3. Mikhail Gorbachev once said, **"If not me, who? And if not now, when?"** In your opinion, what does this quote say about Gorbachev as a person? Your answer should be two to three sentences.

_____

_____

_____

_____

NAME: _____

Nelson Mandela

1. **Match each of the words below with the correct meaning. You may use a dictionary to help you.**

a activist	_____	**A** Found guilty
b resistance	_____	**B** The act of betraying your country
c treason	_____	**C** A person who works for a cause
d convicted	_____	**D** Something that spreads quickly
e epidemic	_____	**E** Fighting against

2. Nelson Mandela fought his country's government. He wanted to allow everyone the right to vote. List **two** reasons why it is important to vote.

a) _____

b) _____

3. Imagine that you were not allowed to vote in your country because of your **race.** Describe how that would make you feel. Give one reason to support your answer.

_____

_____

_____

_____

NAME: _____

Nelson Mandela

 Nelson Mandela was the 11th President of South Africa. He is most famous for being a political **activist.** He worked to end **apartheid.**

The South African government did not allow equal rights for all of their citizens. Mandela began fighting with the **resistance** against the racism he saw. He was arrested twice. He was first put in jail for **treason.** He was arrested for voicing his opinions. He was found not guilty.

STOP

What was Mandela arrested for the first time?

_____

_____

_____

He was arrested a second time. This time, he was **convicted** of organizing an armed attack against the government. He spent twenty-seven years in prison for standing up for what he believed.

His story was famous, and eventually people from around the world put pressure on South Africa. The people of the world wanted Mandela to be freed. The government had to give him his freedom.

After getting out of prison, Mandela made bringing peace to his country his main focus. He worked to give everyone the right to vote. His hard work paid off. He was the first President of South Africa to win an election open to all citizens.

Mandela worked with many human rights groups after he left office. He also worked to fight the AIDS **epidemic** in Africa. He has received the Nobel Peace Prize for his efforts to help end apartheid in South Africa.

Nelson Mandela

1. **Place the following events on the timeline below.**

Events:

a) The world pressures South Africa to free Mandela.

b) Mandela works to stop the AIDS epidemic.

c) Nelson Mandela is convicted and serves twenty-seven years.

d) Mandela is found not guilty of treason.

e) Mandela is elected the 11th President of South Africa.

2. Nelson Mandela once said, **"Education is the most powerful weapon which you can use to change the world."** Explain what this quote means in your own words.

_____

_____

_____

3. How would you **improve** race relations in South Africa? List **three** suggestions.

a) _____

b) _____

c) _____

 Before You Read

Indira Gandhi

1. **Complete each sentence with a word from the list. Use a dictionary to help you.**

surplus	threat	assassinate
export	fraud	

a) Mexico will _____ their fruit and sell it to other countries.

b) It is against the law to _____ a country's leader.

c) Mom made a _____ to take away my computer if my grades do not improve.

d) We have a _____ of tomatoes, so we are giving them to our friends.

e) Because of her earlier _____, I did not believe her when she was telling the truth.

2. Indira Gandhi decided to focus on the problems facing her country. If you were the leader of your country, what **three** problems would you focus on? List them below.

a) _____

b) _____

c) _____

3. Select **one** of the problems you listed above. In a sentence, describe one way you would try to **solve** the problem.

_____

_____

_____

Indira Gandhi

Indira Gandhi was elected the Prime Minister of India two times. Her father, Jawaharlal Nehru, was the Prime Minister years before she became India's leader. She was one of the first women to be an elected leader of a country.

India was in very bad shape when Gandhi took over as leader. She decided to focus on her country rather than global concerns. India was a very poor country and there was not enough food for everyone in the country. Gandhi helped turn a food **shortage** in India into a food **surplus.** India started to **export** their surplus to other countries to make money.

Gandhi started building more nuclear weapons. She thought that both China and Pakistan were **threats** to India. Problems between India and Pakistan became very bad. Gandhi led an eleven-month war against Pakistan. The war ended when Russia helped India and Pakistan reach a peaceful agreement.

STOP

Why did Gandhi start building nuclear weapons?

_____

_____

_____

During Gandhi's leadership, she worked well with Russian leaders. She also met with leaders from the United States, United Kingdom, and Bangladesh.

Indira Gandhi was thought by some people to have committed election **fraud.** A religious group wanted her to step down. She had her army attack the Golden Temple. This is the religious group's holiest place of worship.

This angered the religious group even more. She was **assassinated** by two of her guards who were members of this group. She is remembered for improving the quality of life for Indian citizens.

After You Read

Indira Gandhi

1. Indira Gandhi was a leader who worked in the best interest of her country. Use the reading passage to find **two** examples that show Gandhi had India's best interests at heart.

   a) _____

   _____

   b) _____

   _____

2. In your own words, explain why Indira Gandhi was **assassinated.** Your answer should be three to four sentences.

   _____

   _____

   _____

   _____

   _____

3. What choice would you make if you were Indira Gandhi? Would you choose to leave your job, or would you stay and fight? Give one reason to support your answers.

   _____

   _____

   _____

   _____

 Before You Read

NAME: _____

Yasser Arafat

1. **Write each word from the list beside its correct meaning. Use a dictionary to help you.**

figure	rightfully	hostage	liberation	notable

a) _____ Belonging to

b) _____ Freedom

c) _____ A person held against their wishes by another person

d) _____ A well-known person

e) _____ Famous

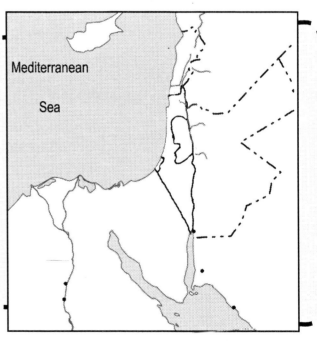

Mediterranean

Sea

2. **On the map to the right, find Israel and Palestine. Using your colored pencils, follow these directions.**

a) Color Palestine **blue.**

b) Color Israel **green.**

3. **Using the resources in your classroom, write down *four facts* about Israel.**

a) _____

b) _____

c) _____

d) _____

NAME: _____

Yasser Arafat

 asser Arafat is a controversial **figure** in world politics. Some people believe he is a freedom fighter. Other people believe that he is a terrorist.

Arafat first received the world's attention because of his connection to the PLO, or the Palestine **Liberation** Organization. This is a group that wanted to force the Jewish people out of Israel. The PLO believed that Israel was **rightfully** part of Palestine. They wanted Israel returned to Palestine.

STOP

Why did the PLO want Israel returned to Palestine?

_____

_____

_____

The PLO was involved in several acts of terrorism. One of the most **notable** happened at the Munich Olympics. At the Olympics, terrorists stormed Olympic village and killed two Israeli athletes. Then, they kidnapped nine other athletes and held them as **hostages.** They wanted 200 Palestinian prisoners released from Israeli prisons. The nine Israeli athletes were killed.

Yasser Arafat was a leader in the PLO at the time of the Munich Olympics. He was **linked** to other terrorist activities through the years. However, as he got older, Arafat decided to work for peace.

Arafat worked with leaders from the U.S. and Israel on a peace agreement. The agreement helped end the fighting between Israel and Palestine.

Many people now see Arafat as a leader who was interested in world peace. He was awarded the Nobel Peace Prize because of the peace agreement he signed with Israel.

Yasser Arafat

1. In your own words, explain why people had different **opinions** about Yasser Arafat. Use one example from the passage to support your answer.

_____

_____

_____

2. Arafat once said, **"I come bearing an olive branch in one hand, and the freedom fighter's gun in the other. Do not let the olive branch fall from my hand."**

What **conclusions** can you draw about Arafat's state of mind at the time? In other words, how did he feel about his decision?

_____

_____

_____

3. Imagine the peace agreement between Palestine and Israel had never been signed. **Predict** how the world would be different if the agreement had never happened.

_____

_____

_____

4. Arafat completely changed his approach. Why do you think Arafat chose to work peacefully?

_____

_____

_____

Jiang Zemin

1. **Match each of the words below with the correct meaning. You may use a dictionary to help you.**

a	Decade	_____	**A**	Country
b	Roles	_____	**B**	A period of ten years
c	Commission	_____	**C**	Value
d	Nation	_____	**D**	Jobs or duties
e	Standard	_____	**E**	The permission to perform certain jobs

2. China's Jiang Zemin was a Communist leader. Identify **two** other Communist leaders you have learned about previously.

a) _____

b) _____

3. **Over one billion** people live in China. Imagine one billion people living in your country. List **three** ways your country would be different.

a) _____

_____

b) _____

_____

c) _____

_____

Jiang Zemin

Jiang Zemin served as a leader of the Communist Party in China for several **decades.** His different leadership **roles** include General Secretary of the Communist Party, President of the People's Republic of China, and Chairman of the Central Military **Commission.**

China was struggling before Zemin took office. He helped China become a much wealthier **nation.** People in China now have a higher **standard** of living. They also have many more personal freedoms.

One major change Zemin led changed politics in China. He allowed private business owners to be members of the Communist Party. This allowed more people to become directly involved with the government.

How did Zemin change politics in China?

STOP

_____

_____

_____

Zemin became very involved in world politics. He spoke several **foreign** languages and liked learning about different cultures. China's relationships with other countries improved.

Zemin visited the U.S. and spoke with President Clinton. Clinton later visited Zemin in China. Before this happened, China and the U.S. had a difficult relationship.

Zemin also brought China into the World Trade Organization. This also helped China become more involved in the world.

China got Hong Kong and Macao back from England and Portugal during Zemin's **term.** He **negotiated** with European leaders to give ownership back to China. He also put in a successful bid for China to host the Summer Olympics before he left office.

Jiang Zemin

1. List the **three** political jobs held by Jiang Zemin.

    a) _____

    b) _____

    c) _____

2. Five changes are listed below. Four are changes made by Zemin. Circle the **four** changes by Jiang Zemin.

    China will host the Summer Olympics.

    Private business owners can participate in the Communist party.

    The relationship between the US and China improves.

    Hong Kong and Macao are turned over to European countries.

    China becomes involved in the World Trade Organization

3. Jiang Zemin was one of the first Chinese leaders to talk with the media. Imagine you are a reporter. List **four questions** you would ask Zemin about his career.

    a) _____

    b) _____

    c) _____

    d) _____

4. Think about the **changes** made by Jiang Zemin. Why did these changes make China a better, stronger country? Your answer should be two to three sentences.

    _____

    _____

    _____

The Dalai Lama

1. **Write each word from the list beside its correct meaning. Use a dictionary to help you.**

| reincarnated | asylum | waste | groomed | restore |

a) _____   To bring back

b) _____   Scraps or leftovers

c) _____   Brought back to life in another body

d) _____   A safe place

e) _____   Made ready for

2. **The map shows both China and Tibet. Use your colored pencils to follow the directions.**

   a) Color Tibet **red.**

   b) Color China **green.**

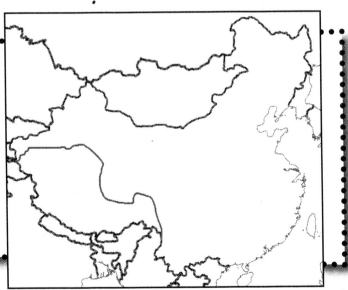

3. ***Three* other world leaders you have read about have been awarded the *Nobel Peace Prize*. List the names of those three leaders below.**

   a) _____

   b) _____

   c) _____

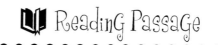

The Dalai Lama

 Tenzin Gyatso is the 14th Dalai Lama. He is the head of state and spiritual leader of Tibet. The Dalai Lama is also called His Holiness. He is the main leader of the Buddhist religion.

The Dalai Lama was discovered to be the **reincarnated** spirit of the last Dalai Lama at the age of two. He was **groomed** to be the Dalai Lama during his childhood.

How did Tenzin Gyatso become the Dalai Lama?

_____

_____

_____

He took over as the Dalai Lama after Chinese soldiers invaded Tibet. The Dalai Lama tried to work out a peaceful solution with China. He was not successful. His Holiness had to **flee** to India where he was given political **asylum.**

The Dalai Lama worked to get his country back from China. He went to the United Nations for help. This was not successful either.

The Five Point Peace Plan was created by the Dalai Lama. He wanted to establish Tibet as a free zone. He wanted to **restore** personal freedoms taken away by the Chinese invaders. He wanted to stop the building of nuclear weapons in Tibet. China was dumping nuclear **waste** in Tibet, and the Dalai Lama wanted that to end. He also wanted to open discussions about freeing Tibet.

China did not agree to the plan. However, the Dalai Lama was **recognized** for his efforts. He was awarded the Nobel Peace Prize for his work to free Tibet and help people around the world.

NAME: _____

The Dalai Lama

1. The Dalai Lama created a Five Point Peace Plan in order to work peacefully with China. List the five points below.

   a) _____

   b) _____

   c) _____

   d) _____

   e) _____

2. Why do you think Dalai Lamas are found when they are children? Explain your opinion in two to three sentences.

   _____

   _____

   _____

3. How would you design a peace plan with China? List **two original points** your plan would include.

   a) _____

   b) _____

4. The Dalai Lama cannot safely return to his country. Describe how you would feel if you could not return to your country. Describe how you would handle the situation. Your answer should be two to three sentences.

   _____

   _____

   _____

Writing Tasks

1. Think about what you have learned about Ronald Reagan, Margaret Thatcher, and Mikhail Gorbachev. Use the Compare and Contrast Pyramid found on page 44. Describe how the leaders are different from each other in the outside triangles. Explain how they are similar in the inside pyramid. Use the graphic organizer in order to write a four paragraph essay.

2. Imagine what the world would be like if The Cold War did not end. Write a four paragraph description of how you think the world would be different.

3. Select one of the countries you have just studied. Write a one-page research paper about your country, including the capital, government, agriculture, industry, and history. You may use the Internet and library to help you.

4. Yasser Arafat worked to end fighting in the Middle East, but his plan did not work for long. Write a one-page peace plan for the Middle East. Include any ideas you have for ending the violence and getting leaders together to talk.

5. Use the Snapshots Organizer on page 45 to summarize the Perons' rise to power. Use supporting details from the reading passage to help you. Your summary should be one to two paragraphs.

6. Several of the leaders you have learned about made decisions that changed their country and the world. Select one leader you have studied. Evaluate their decisions and choices. Do you agree with their decisions? Would you have made the same choices?

Compare and Contrast Pyramid

Using the Pyramid below, describe how Reagan, Thatcher, and Gorbachev are similar to and different from each other.

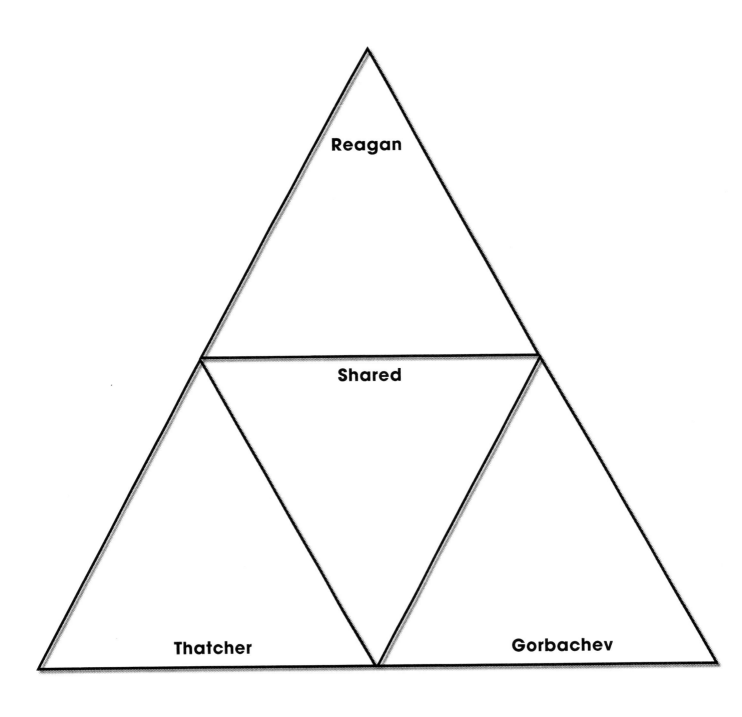

Snapshots Organizer

List the steps taken by the Perons, in the proper order, to achieve and keep power. Write one step in each snapshot below.

NAME: _____

Crossword Puzzle!

Across

1. The first President of the Soviet Union

3. U.S. President who helped end Cold War

7. U.S. President who declared a war on terrorism

9. Argentinian leader who worked to help poor

10. Spiritual leader of Tibet

12. In prison for over 20 years for what he believed

13. Made drug laws more strict in Mexico

Down

1. Worked to improve conditions in India

2. Close ally with Russian leaders during Cold War

4. Weapons

6. To let go

7. Made ready for

8. Chinese leader who helped China become more involved in World Politics

10. Known as "The Iron Lady" in the United Kingdom

11. A former leader of the PLO who worked for peace in the Middle East

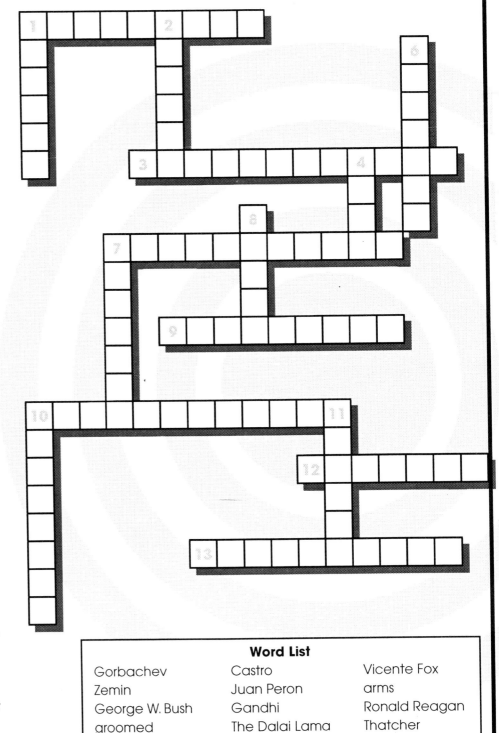

Word List

Gorbachev	Castro	Vicente Fox
Zemin	Juan Peron	arms
George W. Bush	Gandhi	Ronald Reagan
groomed	The Dalai Lama	Thatcher
release	Arafat	Mandela

NAME: _____

 After You Read

Word Search

Find all of the words in the Word Search. Words are written horizontally, vertically, diagonally, and some are even written backwards.

t	e	r	t	f	u	i	s	o	l	a	t	e	d	i	y	d	a
e	e	b	k	c	o	n	f	l	i	c	t	w	i	h	t	k	p
r	u	r	a	r	g	y	v	d	m	g	c	k	a	n	i	c	a
m	y	t	r	e	a	s	o	n	g	j	b	e	a	l	k	a	r
r	g	n	h	o	s	f	d	e	c	a	d	e	w	t	t	j	t
l	o	a	w	s	r	h	o	w	t	m	h	a	d	h	p	h	h
i	t	l	a	e	g	i	t	e	g	o	y	j	f	d	u	g	e
d	k	l	d	g	j	s	s	n	s	u	m	m	i	t	r	i	i
e	r	i	f	e	u	v	c	t	w	f	t	j	d	l	r	h	d
l	k	e	h	l	q	e	a	d	c	o	u	r	s	e	o	t	i
f	c	s	p	d	w	g	z	x	t	u	s	c	h	p	c	w	e
a	f	r	x	m	e	x	p	o	r	t	h	q	e	i	l	d	t
c	u	r	e	c	o	n	o	m	y	h	u	e	t	q	e	i	k
s	c	r	o	w	t	o	j	d	r	y	c	i	g	k	w	r	e
t	h	r	e	a	t	e	a	e	y	u	z	p	n	l	o	h	e
w	d	u	g	l	s	r	s	h	g	e	p	i	d	e	m	i	c
a	o	j	i	a	d	g	u	k	n	v	l	n	r	m	y	e	l
l	y	g	e	e	a	d	u	s	c	z	f	i	m	o	n	f	k
s	k	l	s	w	e	a	l	t	h	y	u	i	s	s	r	h	s
n	e	r	y	e	g	k	y	f	a	d	i	k	j	d	e	e	e
r	r	l	i	b	e	r	a	t	i	o	n	a	r	g	o	y	s
i	f	y	r	t	p	e	r	s	o	n	a	b	l	e	u	o	i
r	e	i	n	c	a	r	n	a	t	e	d	k	f	g	y	e	g

terrorist	summit	reincarnated	release
term	aid	export	threat
hostage	corrupt	conflict	economy
treason	epidemic	fled	goods
apartheid	linked	allies	wealthy
isolated	surplus	highjack	personable
citizens	decade	course	liberation

World Political Leaders CC5761

After You Read 📖 NAME: _____

Comprehension Quiz

25

5

1. Circle the word **TRUE** if the statement is TRUE **or** Circle the word **FALSE** if it is FALSE.

   a) Yasser Arafat always worked for peace in the Middle East.

       TRUE   **FALSE**

   b) China has allowed the Dalai Lama to return to Tibet to lead.

       TRUE   **FALSE**

   c) Thatcher, Reagan, and Gorbachev worked to end the Cold War.

       TRUE   **FALSE**

   d) Indira Gandhi created a food shortage in India.

       TRUE   **FALSE**

   e) Mandela helped apartheid spread in South Africa.

       TRUE   **FALSE**

Part B

Match the leader on the left with their actions on the right.

5

1	**Bush**	A	Organized the Rainbow Tour to meet with other world leaders	
2	**Mandela**	B	Worked with Bush on immigration	
3	**The Perons**	C	Took over his country after a coup	
4	**Fox**	D	Invaded Iraq	
5	**Castro**	E	Worked to end the AIDS epidemic in Africa	

SUBTOTAL: /10

World Political Leaders CC5761

After You Read 📖

Comprehension Quiz

Part C

Answer the questions in complete sentences.

1. Explain how **Reagan** helped end the Cold War. Give examples when answering. ③

_____

_____

2. Explain how **Eva Peron** was different from other women leaders. Give examples when answering. ③

_____

_____

3. Explain how **Zemin** helped China become more involved in world politics. Give examples when answering. ③

_____

_____

4. Explain why people have different opinions on **Yasser Arafat**. Give examples when answering. ③

_____

_____

5. Why did the **Dalai Lama** create the Five Point Peace Plan? Give two examples when answering. ③

_____

_____

_____

SUBTOTAL: /15

1.

a) Castro takes over
b) Works with Russia
c) Ends relationship with Russia
d) Encourages tourism

2. Answers will vary

3. Answers will vary

4. Answers will vary

⑮

1.

a) oppose
b) personable
c) aid
d) dictator
e) isolated
f) embargo
g) hostile

2. Answers will vary

3. Answers will vary

⑬

Cuba and Russia could attack

⑭

Arms reduction treaties

⑪

1.

(Arms race begins)
(President visits Russia)
(Arms reduction treaties)

2. Answers will vary

3. Answers will vary

4. Answers will vary

⑫ Answers will vary

1.

a) D
b) E
c) B
d) A
e) F
f) C

2. Answers will vary

3. Answers will vary

⑩ Answers will vary

1.

a) FALSE
b) TRUE
c) FALSE
d) TRUE

2.

Events in order from left to right:

c) September 11, 2001,
d) Troops sent to Afghanistan,
e) Troops sent to Iraq,
b) Hussein guilty,
a) Elections

3. Answers will vary

⑨

1.

a) disbanding
b) conflict
c) terrorist
d) overthrow
e) course
f) controversial
g) highjack

2.

U.S. should be colored red

Afghanistan should be colored blue

Iraq should be colored green

⑦

Overthrow the Taliban

⑧

1.
a) Brought leaders together

b) End apartheid; free Mandela

2. Answers will vary

3. Answers will vary

1.
a) release
b) published
c) apartheid
d) allies
e) negotiated

2. England, Northern Ireland, Scotland, and Wales.

3. England, Northern Ireland, Scotland, and Wales should be labelled.

Nelson Mandela

1.
a) Eliminate poverty
b) Give power to working class

2. To meet with other leaders

3. Answers will vary

4. Answers will vary

1.
a) organization
b) eliminate
c) linked
d) wealthy
e) fled
f) recognized
g) ambitious

2. Answers will vary

Did not want to share wealth

1.
Works with Bush and Castro
Talk about immigration
Drugs in Mexico

2.
a) Coca-Cola
b) Should not get involved
c) To control immigration

3. Answers will vary

1.
a — C
b — E
c — A
d — F
e — D
f — B

2.
U.S. should be colored red
Cuba should be colored blue
Mexico should be colored green

Corruption and drugs

1.
a) Created food surplus
b) Sold surplus for money

2. Answers will vary

3. Answers will vary

(33)

1.
a) export
b) assassinate
c) threat
d) surplus
e) fraud

2. Answers will vary

3. Answers will vary

(31)

(32) Thought China and Pakistan were threats

1.

Events in order from left to right:

Not guilty of treason,
Serves 27 years,
World pressures South Africa,
11th President,
Works to stop AIDS epidemic

2. Answers will vary

3. Answers will vary

(30)

1.
a) C
b) E
c) B
d) A
e) D

2. Answers will vary

3. Answers will vary

(28)

(29) Treason

1.
a) FALSE
b) TRUE
c) FALSE
d) TRUE
e) TRUE

2. Answers will vary

3. Answers will vary

(27)

1.
a) goods
b) coup
c) shortage
d) collapsed
e) citizens

2. Answers will vary

3. Answers will vary

U.S.
United Kingdom
Cuba

(25)

(26) Let people own businesses

Across:

1. Gorbachev

3. Ronald Reagan

7. George W. Bush

9. Juan Peron

10. The Dalai Lama

12. Mandela

13. Vicente Fox

Down:

1. Gandhi

2. Castro

4. arms

6. release

7. groomed

8. Zemin

10. Thatcher

11. Arafat

1.
a) Tibet a free zone
b) Restore freedoms
c) Stop nuclear weapons
d) End dumping waste
e) Open talks with China

2. Answers will vary

3. Answers will vary

4. Answers will vary

(42)

All answers will vary

(43)

1.
a) restore
b) waste
c) reincarnated
d) asylum
e) groomed

2. Tibet should be colored red, China should be colored green

3.
a) Gorbachev
b) Mandela
c) Arafat

(40)

Found at age 2

(41)

Business owners could be members

(38)

1.
a) General Secretary
b) President
c) Chairman of Central Military Commission

2.
Host Olympics
Business owners in party
Relationship improves
World Trade Organization

3. Answers will vary

4. Answers will vary

(39)

All Answers will vary

(36)

1.
a — B
b — D
c — E
d — A
e — C

2.
a) Fidel Castro
b) Mikhail Gorbachev

3. Answers will vary

(37)

1.
a) rightfully
b) liberation
c) hostage
d) figure
e) notable

2. Palestine should be colored blue, Israel should be colored green

3. Answers will vary

(34)

Israel was part of Palestine

(35)

(46)

Word Search Answers

Part A

a) **FALSE**

b) **FALSE**

c) **TRUE**

d) **FALSE**

e) **FALSE**

Part B

1 D

2 E

3 A

4 B

5 C

(48)

Part C

1. Faced problem; Examples will vary

2. Active in politics; Examples will vary

3. Examples will vary

4. Terrorist or peacemaker; Examples will vary

5. Wanted to free Tibet; Examples will vary

(49)

(47)

World Map

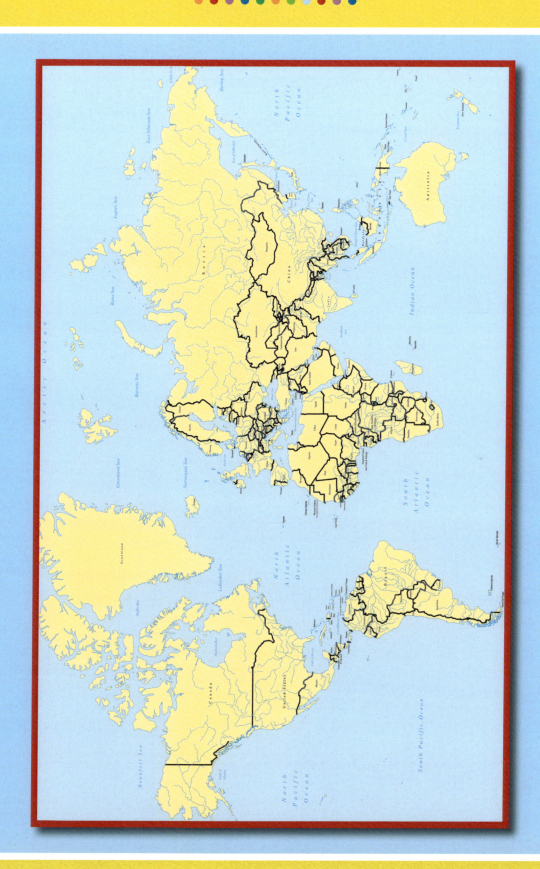

 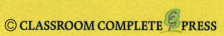

Berlin Wall

Before

After

Cold war cause and effect chart

Cause

Reagan starts arms race

Thatcher tells Reagan that Gorbachev can be worked with.

Reagan tells Gorbachev to tear down Berlin Wall

Effect

Russia and US sign arms reduction treaties

Reagan, Thatcher, and Gorbachev work to end Cold War

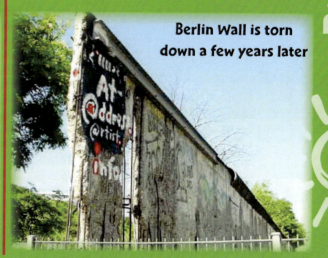
Berlin Wall is torn down a few years later

World Political Leaders CC5761

Map of Palestine

Before

After

Potala Palace
(In Lhasa, Tibet Chief residence of the Dalai Lama)

Flags

Argentina

Mexico

China

Russia

Cuba

United Kingdom

India

United States of America

World Political Leaders CC5761